The Selected
John Hewitt

*edited
with an introduction
by*

Alan Warner

Blackstaff Press

POETRY IRELAND CHOICE
1981

First published in 1981 by
The Blackstaff Press Limited
3 Galway Park, Dundonald, Belfast BT16 0AN, Northern Ireland
with the assistance of
The Arts Council of Northern Ireland
Reprinted 1986, 1988, 1991

Printed by The Guernsey Press Company Limited

British Library Cataloguing in Publication Data
Hewitt, John
The selected John Hewitt.
I. Title   II. Warner, Alan
821'.912   PR6015.E778
ISBN 0-85640-244-3

Contents

Introduction

John Harold Hewitt was born at 96 Cliftonpark Avenue in Belfast on 28 October 1907. His father, Robert Telford Hewitt (1873–1945), was a teacher who became Principal of Agnes Street Mixed School, a National School attached to Agnes Street Methodist Church, which was built in 1886 near the Shankill Road. His mother was Elinor Robinson, who had also been a teacher for a time. A small woman but a redoubtable walker, she pushed her young son in his pram for long regular outings. Perhaps it was this early experience that gave him a strong love of country air.

On both sides his ancestors were devout Methodists. The Robinsons who came from Wolfhill, a small village near Belfast, were caught up in the fever of religious revival that reached its peak in 1859, the 'Year of Grace'. His father's family came from Kilmore in County Armagh, where they seem to have been settled for several centuries. The name Hewitt is English in origin, but there were some links with Scotland. The poet's grandfather moved to Scotland for a time and his father, Robert Telford Hewitt, was born in Glasgow. John Hewitt recalls a Scots timbre in his father's speech on the telephone.

Although Robert Telford Hewitt was liberal in his outlook in many ways, his strong non-conformist background gave him certain rigidities. In his steadfast disapproval of alcohol he was uncompromising and un-Irish. His own father had resigned from his Orange Lodge when it was agreed to permit the consumption of strong drink. Robert Hewitt, a lifelong abstainer, actually returned the wedding presents that were sent to him by the wealthiest of his mother's relatives, who had some connection with the liquor trade. This stern adherence to principle caused a resentment that lasted for many years. John Hewitt did not himself follow the family tradition

1

of teetotalism, but he remained a very modest drinker, content mostly with a single glass, and he reflects a little ruefully on 'the vigorous element of teetotalism which still has power to nudge my elbow in any bar'. (*The Bell*, Jan. 1953: 'Planter's Gothic' by John Howard)

His grandfather boasted that 'no Hewitt ever married a Papist or kept a public-house'. Hewitt did not break with family tradition in either of these ways, but when he was twelve he made friends with a Catholic boy of his own age, when a new family moved into the house next door. This friend lent him his magazine, *Our Boys*, which opened up a new world to his imagination. It 'carried exciting stories of Cuchullain and Colmcille and Red Hugh O'Donnell and Owen Roe O'Neill and the Penal Days and the Famine... So began my fifty years' involvement in the story of our country's past and the rights and wrongs of it.' The family moved and it was some years before Hewitt acquired another Catholic friend, a fellow-undergraduate at the university, 'an amusing anti-clerical young man'. (*Threshold*, no. 23, 1970)

By an odd quirk of chance Hewitt escaped baptism into the Methodist Church, because his father disliked the local Minister who was in charge at the time his baptism was due, and in any case he attached little importance to that formal rite. His son later appreciated the symbolic freedom from church and creed that this omission had given him.

> This has given me a sense of liberation, spiritually I have felt myself to be my own man, the ultimate Protestant. And when to this I add the fact that since our family doctor, a friendly old man in a frock-coat and with a pointed beard, had no great belief in vaccination, and going through the secular ritual with me, deliberately used an innocuous concoction, which left no scar, I have often felt doubly free from the twin disciplines of organised religion and science.
>
> (*The Bell*, Autumn 1953)

Hewitt's reading and thinking soon carried him away from the Methodist Church, and although he tried hard to appreciate the virtues of John Wesley, the father of Methodism, he could never warm to him.

How I wish I could like that man more. Each time a new biography appears I take it up hoping to find some basis for the respect I am compelled to feel for so earnest and indefatigable a worker, so effective and inspiring a preacher; but each time I am defeated and lay down the volume respectfully, but without any love. So, for me, it is George Fox every time, the man in leather breeches, who doffed his hat to no steeplehouse. William Blake, too, is of that company, and St Francis of Assisi. And, weighing as fairly as I can, even compensating liberally for my acknowledged prejudice, the astonishing virtues of Wesley and his long life of devoted service to his personal vision against a single gesture by Fox, or a drawing by Blake, I am forced reluctantly to mark him off with Calvin and St Paul and Knox and Aquinas and Augustine and Luther as outside my myth.

(*The Bell*, Autumn 1953)

Unbaptised, improperly vaccinated, enquiring and agnostic, Hewitt was to fashion his own myth out of diverse elements. But though he turned away from his parents' church and creed, he retained a protestant and puritan temper, and he held firmly to the radical side of the non-conformist tradition and its strong feeling for social justice.

He began his education in his father's school in Agnes Street, and continued it at Methodist College. Afterwards he went on to Queen's University, where he took a degree in English. He wrote an M.A. thesis on 'Ulster Poets, 1800–1870'. Later on he was to use some of the material he collected at this time in his book *Rhyming Weavers, and other country poets of Antrim and Down*. In 1930 he was appointed Art Assistant at the Belfast Museum and Art Gallery, and he stayed here until 1957, in due course becoming Deputy Director.

Apart from his job he had a strong natural interest in painting and in the arts generally. He made friends with two young painters, William J. McClughin and John Luke. Like Wordsworth and his friends, these young men moved in a world of plain living and high thinking, which illustrates aptly the puritan temper I have spoken of. In his book on John Luke, Hewitt writes: 'It was not in any appreciable measure due to their economic circumstances that my friends were frugal, abstemious and celibate. In our protracted debates and disputations our reason was never clouded nor our arts given a seeming brilliance by alcohol, and I was the only serious smoker in the company.' The pub, the background of so much intellectual and artistic life in Ireland, does not figure largely in Hewitt's world.

His thinking and reading took him further in the radical direction that the non-conformist tradition had pointed him. It was his father, he says, who 'set the leaping flame/ of social justice in my wayward heart'. In the kitchen of the Hewitt home there were photographs of Keir Hardie and Jim Larkin. He read about and admired many English radical thinkers and writers. He cites 'John Ball, the Diggers, the Levellers, the Chartists, Paine, Cobbett, Morris' (*Aquarius*, no. 5, 1972). William Morris, in particular, exercised a strong influence on him because he offered the hope of combining a social revolution with an aesthetic one. In *News from Nowhere* Morris dreamed of a new-old society where men turned away from machines and money, and worked with their hands, making beautiful and useful things in happiness and innocence. To Morris's influence was added that of Karl Marx. 'It was a dead German Jew who gave me my guide-lines. It was an English poet, who for me, most movingly evoked the quality of the Good Society in his *News from Nowhere*' (*Aquarius*). In the Thirties Hewitt found his affinities were with the Labour Party and the Left Book Club.

In 1934 he married Roberta Black, who also lived in Belfast. His wife shared his political sympathies and they were both active in the Belfast Peace League. She was the secretary of this group, which hoped to do something to counter the growing threats of war, and he was on the committee. They both became involved also with the National Council of Civil Liberties, which was investigating the Special Powers Act, 'that very idiosyncratic piece of Stormont legislation'. Hewitt referred to this episode many years later in the article he wrote for *Aquarius*, 'No rootless colonist', from which I have been quoting.

> My interest was that this was a reactionary repressive weapon, to be criticised in any context where democratic values were respected. So my wife – I was just married – and I, with R.M. Henry and Alexander MacBeath, Professors of the University, engaged ourselves in preliminary investigation to pilot the Council's examination. This was my first acquaintance with

the nature of state authority and its techniques of the opened letter and the tapped telephone.

But Hewitt was not only active in political directions. In 1934 he helped to form a progressive art group, known as the 'Ulster Unit'. This group was formed on the model of 'Unit One' in England, a group of English painters, sculptors and architects, which included Paul Nash, Ben Nicholson, Barbara Hepworth and Henry Moore. The 'Ulster Unit' included John Luke, George McCann and Colin Middleton, and an exhibition was mounted to stimulate an interest in contemporary art.

At the same time Hewitt was writing poetry and coming to the decision that poetry was to be an important part of his life's work. He began to get poems published in a number of periodicals. His work appeared in the *Irish Statesman* in 1929, and later in *The Listener*, the *New Statesman*, *Adelphi*, *The Times Literary Supplement*, the *Irish Times*, *Poetry Ireland* and other periodicals and anthologies, but much of what he wrote did not appear in print until many years later.

In the Forties he was strongly influenced by the concept of Regionalism. This has something in common with current notions that 'small is beautiful'. In a vast, bureaucratic, centralised world, the idea that meaning and significance might be sought in a limited region, with its local history and traditions and special characteristics, seemed attractive. Ulster offered itself as an obvious regional choice, and other writers and artists shared Hewitt's views. An Ulster literary annual, entitled *Lagan*, was launched, to which Hewitt contributed. This local enthusiasm lasted for some years, but eventually the phase ended and the wider world returned.

Meanwhile Hewitt had become Deputy Director of the Museum and Art Gallery, and when the Director retired it was natural that he should expect to be appointed to this post. But in the event his liberal and socialist sympathies were held against him. The Unionist Chairman of the Committee responsible for the appointment, as Hewitt ruefully recounted later, insisted that 'besides being a Communist I had numerous Catholic friends, play-actors and the like' (*Threshold*, no. 23, 1970). So he moved away from Belfast for a time to take a post as Art Director of the Herbert Art Gallery and Museum in Coventry. He liked many aspects of life there, and he enjoyed walking in the English countryside and visiting places of historic interest, but his thoughts were often across the Irish Sea, and when he retired in 1972 he returned to Belfast. In a poem referring to his 'exile', he rejects the thought of comparing himself with Dante, exiled from Florence, but ends

> ...and then there was return—
> as some translated poet wrote—
> *to this betraying, violent city*
> *irremediably home.*
>
> ('1957–1972': *The Rain Dance*)

Hewitt is inescapably an Ulsterman and for him Belfast is 'irremediably home', and yet much of his life and his poetry has been a search for identity. He claims an Irish heritage that includes the whole of Ireland and the whole Irish past, as the first part of this selection demonstrates. He found an apt symbol for his sense of inheriting the older Irish traditions when he discovered that the Planter's Gothic tower of Kilmore church, the church of his ancestors, still enclosed the stump of a round tower, and that it was built on the site of a Culdee holy place. 'It is the best symbol I have yet found for the strange textures of my response to this island of which I am a native. I may appear Planter's Gothic, but there is a round tower somewhere inside, and needled through every sentence I utter.'

Later, in a symposium in the *Irish Times* (4 July 1974), he defined his position clearly:

> I'm an Ulsterman, of planter stock. I was born in the island of Ireland, so secondarily I'm an Irishman. I was born in the British archipelago and English is my native tongue, so I am British. The British archipelago consists of offshore islands to the continent of Europe, so I'm European. This is my hierarchy of values and so far as I am concerned, anyone who omits one step in that sequence of values is falsifying the situation.

In his retirement John Hewitt has continued to write and publish. Since 1974 the Blackstaff Press have published four collections of his poetry, and yet another is forthcoming. In 1974 he was awarded an honorary D.Litt. by the New University of Ulster, and from 1976 to 1979 he was Writer in Residence at his old university, Queen's, in Belfast. Now in his seventies, he faces old age with calm dignity, still reading and writing and thinking, still serving on committees, still ready to talk to friends and strangers. As he says in 'Expectancy', the last poem of this selection, he waits for the breaking light of eternity as one still engaged in the patient labours of time.

> I wait here for this light in my own fashion,
> not lonely on a rock against the sky,
> but as the men who bred me, in their day,
> as men in country places still, have time,
> working in some long field, to answer you.

In an early essay on Hewitt's poetry (*Poetry Ireland*, no. 3, Spring 1964) John Montague described him as 'the first (and probably the last) deliberately Ulster, Protestant poet'. We have already seen how his life and background made him take a strong and deliberate stand as an Ulsterman, and this is clearly revealed in his poetry; but it is less easy to see him as a deliberately Protestant poet, especially if 'Protestant' is spelt with a capital 'P'. His bent of mind is protestant in the radical and doubting sense, and it moves him away from churches and creeds. At the same time his non-conformist upbringing made him unsympathetic to the Roman Catholic faith. This is apparent in 'The Glens', where he voices his suspicion of that 'vainer creed' and says, 'I fear the lifted hand against unfettered thought.'

Yet it would be wholly wrong to think of Hewitt's poetry as the voice of Protestant Ulster. What comes through most clearly is his detachment and loneliness. Spiritually his own man, the ultimate protestant with a small 'p', he is aware of his separation from the group, the community, the tribe. *I found myself alone* was the title given to a short film of his life and work made by the Arts Council of Northern Ireland in 1978, and this indicates a leading motif in his personality and his poetry. The title was taken from a line in one of his own poems, 'Because I paced my thought'. In this poem he finds himself alone in the city world of political debate because he paced his thought by the natural world. But in the country also he frequently found himself alone. He is acutely conscious of his difference from the people of the hill farms, and he expresses it forcibly in the poem 'O country people'.

7

I would be neighbourly, would come to terms
with your existence, but you are so far;
there is a wide bog between us, a high wall.
I've tried to learn the smaller parts of speech
in your slow language, but my thoughts need more
flexible shapes to move in, if I am to reach
into the hearth's red heart across the half-door.

To some extent a poet must always be an outsider, a watcher, whether in a field or in a city street. The nature of his activity makes him an observer, standing to one side, rather than a man caught up in the life of a farm or a factory. Although Hewitt was troubled by the gap between himself and the country people, he nevertheless observes the life of the countryside with love and sympathy.

Alone in many ways, he is still bound to Ulster by strong pieties of place, of family and local history. *Kites in Spring*, his latest collection of poems, celebrates a Belfast boyhood, and shows how important in his emotional development were his home, his family circle and the streets of Belfast. It is interesting to observe the sharp contrast revealed by the attitude of another twentieth-century poet to his native place. Philip Larkin was born in Coventry, but for him the town has little or no emotional significance. In a poem entitled ironically 'I remember, I remember' (*The Less Deceived*, 1955), Larkin writes of passing through his birthplace by train and looking at it with detachment and disappointment.

'Was that,' my friend smiled, 'where you "have your roots"?'
'No, only where my childhood was unspent,'
I wanted to retort, 'just where I started...'

Larkin seems to deny any possibility or necessity of roots in place or past, but for Hewitt these roots are a vital source of his poetic imagination. Even though he abandoned the deliberate cult of Regionalism as a programme for writers and artists, he retained a strong sense of place and a strong feeling for the past, in Ulster and in Ireland generally. He is aware of his kinship with earlier Ulster writers, like William Allingham, and even those simple 'rhyming weavers', whose little books of verse he collected and cherished. Although he has lived outside Ireland and travelled widely in Europe,

8

he still thinks of himself as a local poet, whose first allegiance is to places and people in the north of Ireland. 'A local poet' is the title he gives the ironic, self-deprecating poem on page 113 where 'he mourns for his mannerly verses/that had left so much unsaid'.

The Belfast boyhood and the non-conformist background that helped to shape Hewitt's temperament and the themes of his poetry may be seen also to have influenced his style and manner of writing. There is often a deliberate plainness in the language he uses that has misled some readers into thinking him dull and prosaic, lacking in colour. Though he avoids rhetoric and display, and his preference is for spare, controlled statement, there is considerable variety and range in his poetry. Sometimes the quiet, unemphatic tone conceals reserves of power. At a first reading it is easy to miss the subtleties and ironies that give edge to some poems. The reader needs to be alert and responsive, and to take careful note of the advice given by the poet himself in the introductory poem to Section IV of this selection, 'I write for...'.

> I write for my own kind,
> I do not pitch my voice
> that every phrase be heard
> by those who have no choice...

The poem 'Frost', which will be found in Section 3, provides a good example of the way his poetry works. At first reading it would be easy to pass it by as a pleasing slight sketch of winter, but careful attention to tone and imagery reveals considerable subtlety and insight. The second verse presents a striking image of old age.

> So must the world seem keen and very bright
> to one whose gaze is on the end of things,
> who knows, past summer lush, brimmed autumn's height,
> no promise in the inevitable springs,
> all stripped of shadow down to bone of light,
> the false songs gone and gone the restless wings.

The phrase 'bone of light' in the penultimate line is original and evocative. It suggests a paring down of all growth and texture, all earthy and fleshly covering, down to the hard bony skeleton. At the

9

same time this brings light and illumination. Frost and clear air, the first verse suggests, show us the naked reality of the landscape – 'a tree is truer for its being bare'. We may wish to dispute this point, but the poem makes us vividly aware of the possibility of it, and of the way in which the world might 'seem keen and very bright/to one whose gaze is on the end of things'.

Because of his skill and care in the choice of words Hewitt can achieve strong effects within narrow limits. In his collection with the intriguing title, *Scissors for a One-Armed Tailor*, he follows the example of early Irish poets who wrote brief marginal lyrics while engaged on lengthy works of translation or copying. We find him condensing a great deal of meaning into two or three simple lines, as in the first verse of 'The romantic'.

> When the first white flakes
> fall out of the black Antrim sky
> I toboggan across Alaska.

The shortest poem in this collection, 'Grey and white', contains only sixteen words, but it catches deftly the mood of a grey day on the Ulster coast.

Although Hewitt has deep roots in Ulster rock and clay, the leaves on his tree of verse breathe freely in an air that circulates round the world. He can bring before us a local scene but he can also face us with a general metaphysical and moral problem, as in 'The child, the chair, the leaf.' In 'Revenant', which is wholly different in mood and manner, he dramatises an age-old mystery. His two 'Sonnets to Roberta' are deeply personal, offering a subtle and severe self-analysis. 'The coasters' is ironical and objective. This book contains only a modest selection of Hewitt's sum total of verse, but the reader will find a wide range of theme and style within it.

It is usual for a selection of poems from a single author to be arranged in chronological order, but in this book I have chosen to group the poems in four sections, corresponding roughly to their themes, though the poems in the last section, 'Memories and thoughts', naturally cover widely divergent topics. I believe that when the poems are grouped in this way they assist one another in revealing the currents of the poet's thoughts and feelings, although it means that the selection begins with some relatively late work.

At the foot of each poem is a note of its source and the date when it was written. The titles of the separately published collections, which provide the sources, have been abbreviated as follows:

Collected Poems, 1932–1967	CP
Kites in Spring	KS
Out of My Time	OMT
The Rain Dance	RD
Scissors for a One-Armed Tailor	SOT
Time Enough	TE
An Ulster Reckoning	UR

1.
An Irish Heritage

Many Ulster people are troubled by doubts about their nationality and heritage. For example, what answer should go down on a printed form under the heading of 'Nationality': British or Irish? Legally and constitutionally the correct answer is British; but how many Ulster people can write this down without a twinge of doubt or hesitation? John Hewitt has a strong sense of Irish identity. Although he was never an Irish speaker, he is deeply read in Irish history and literature, and he has a keen awareness of Irish traditions that stretch far back beyond the partition of Ireland in 1921. He claims kinship with Oisin and St Patrick and Brian Boru. On the very first page of his *Collected Poems* he begins with the words 'We Irish...' and in various ways he repeats the statement made in the lines from 'Conacre' that follow: 'this is my home and country'.

from Conacre

...But neither saint nor fool,
rather a happy man who seldom sees
the emptiness behind the images
that wake my heart to wonder, I derive
sufficient joy from being here alive
in this mad island crammed with bloody ghosts
and moaning memories of forgotten coasts
our fathers steered from, where we cannot go
the names so lost in time's grey undertow.

This is my home and country. Later on
perhaps I'll find this nation is my own
but here and now it is enough to love
this faulted ledge, this map of cloud above,
and the great sea that beats against the west
to swamp the sun.

1943   CP

The Irish dimension

With these folk gone, next door was tenanted
by a mild man, an Army Officer,
two girls, a boy, left in his quiet care,
his wife their mother, being some years dead.
We shortly found that they were Catholics,
the very first I ever came to know;
To other friends they might be Teagues or Micks;
the lad I quickly found no sort of foe.

Just my own age. His Christian Brothers' School
to me seemed cruel. As an altar boy
he served with dread. His magazines were full
of faces, places named, unknown to me.
Benburb, Wolfe Tone, Cuchullain, Fontenoy.
I still am grateful, Willie Morrisey.

1978   KS

16

In the Rosses

The hospitable Irish
come out to see who passes,
bid you sit by the fire
till it is time for mass.

The room is bare, the bed
is shabby in the corner,
but the fine talk is ready
and the wide hearth is warm.

1942   SOT

Gloss: on the difficulties of translation

Across Loch Laig
the yellow-billed blackbird
whistles from the blossomed whin.

Not, as you might expect,
a Japanese poem, although
it has the seventeen
syllables of the *haiku*.
Ninth-century Irish, in fact,
from a handbook on metrics,
the first written reference
to my native place.

In forty years of verse
I have not inched much further.
I may have matched the images;
but the intricate word-play
of the original – assonance
rime, alliteration –
is beyond my grasp.

To begin with, I should
have to substitute
golden for *yellow*
and *gorse* for *whin*,
this last is the word we use
on both sides of Belfast Loch.

1968   OMT

Two Irish saints

1 *St Patrick*

So Patrick once, striding the flogging weathers,
and hoisting hills with fire, took kings to task,
proud only as a man who bears a mask
to glaze his wound against the cynic fingers,
brought Christ to Eire better than the others
who, baffled, oared the yeasty billow's risk,
and grated back on limestone, pale, loquacious;
for he died blest and lies in his own shadow.

Yet loud with Leary, dominant with druids,
passing with stags tall-antlered down the valley,
was happy only when his text-vexed eyes
saw the flat Lough from Slemish as before,
how long ago, the boy stood with the swine,
and dreamt of Christ's bright sandals in the heather.

2 *Colmcille*

Of Colmcille, blood-arrogant and royal,
spilling a war like a flung fist of cards,
throwing his purple round the threatened poets,
and taunting the slow king with lettered vellum,
too much remains within the veins and sinews
of this mad people, turbulent and rash,
the knuckled swift intolerance, the tongue
too ready with the rasped malicious words.

Rather for succour, think of that far island:
the patient fellows singing in the byre,
the small world scooped and narrowed to an Eden,
whence, daily, he would pass, with blessing fingers,
spadesmen, mason, dark man beating metal,
to print the tide's track with his sharpened ribs.

1944   CP

19

Once alien here

Once alien here my fathers built their house,
claimed, drained, and gave the land the shapes of use,
and for their urgent labour grudged no more
than shuffled pennies from the hoarded store
of well rubbed words that had left their overtones
in the ripe England of the moulded downs.

The sullen Irish limping to the hills
bore with them the enchantments and the spells
that in the clans' free days hung gay and rich
on every twig of every thorny hedge,
and gave the rain-pocked stone a meaning past
the blurred engraving of the fibrous frost.

So I, because of all the buried men
in Ulster clay, because of rock and glen
and mist and cloud and quality of air
as native in my thought as any here,
who now would seek a native mode to tell
our stubborn wisdom individual,
yet lacking skill in either scale of song,
the graver English, lyric Irish tongue,
must let this rich earth so enhance the blood
with steady pulse where now is plunging mood
till thought and image may, identified,
find easy voice to utter each aright.

1942   CP

The colony

First came the legions, then the colonists,
provincials, landless citizens, and some
camp-followers of restless generals
content now only with the least of wars.
Among this rabble, some to feel more free
beyond the ready whim of Caesar's fist;
for conscience' sake the best of these, but others
because their debts had tongues, one reckless man,
a tax absconder with a sack of coin.

With these, young lawclerks skilled with chart and stylus,
their boxes crammed with lease-scrolls duly marked
with distances and names, to be defined
when all was mapped.
                              When they'd surveyed the land,
they gave the richer tillage, tract by tract,
from the great captains down to men-at-arms,
some of the sprawling rents to be retained
by Caesar's mistresses in their far villas.

We planted little towns to garrison
the heaving country, heaping walls of earth
and keeping all our cattle close at hand;
then, thrusting north and west, we felled the trees,
selling them off the foot hills, at a stroke
making quick profits, smoking out the nests
of the barbarian tribesmen, clan by clan,
who hunkered in their blankets, biding chance,
till, unobserved, they slither down and run
with torch and blade among the frontier huts
when guards were nodding, or when shining corn
bade sword-hand grip the sickle. There was once
a terrible year when, huddled in our towns,
my people trembled as the beacons ran
from hill to hill across the countryside,
calling the dispossessed to lift their standards.

There was great slaughter then, man, woman, child,
with fire and pillage of our timbered houses;
we had to build in stone for ever after.

That terror dogs us; back of all our thought
the threat behind the dream, those beacons flare,
and we run headlong screaming in our fear;
fear quickened by the memory of guilt
for we began the plunder – naked men
still have their household gods and holy places,
and what a people loves it will defend.
We took their temples from them and forbade them,
for many years, to worship their strange idols.
They gathered secret, deep in the dripping glens,
chanting their prayers before a lichened rock.

We took the kindlier soils. It had been theirs,
this patient, temperate, slow, indifferent,
crop-yielding, crop-denying, in-neglect-
quickly-returning-to-the-nettle-and-bracken,
sodden and friendly land. We took it from them.
We laboured hard and stubborn, draining, planting,
till half the country took its shape from us.

Only among the hills with hare and kestrel,
will you observe what once this land was like
before we made it fat for human use—
all but the forests, all but the tall trees—
I could invent a legend of those trees,
and how their creatures, dryads, hamadryads,
fled from the copses, hid in thorny bushes,
and grew a crooked and malignant folk,
plotting and waiting for a bitter revenge
on their despoilers. So our troubled thought
is from enchantments of the old tree magic,
but I am not a sick and haunted man...

Teams of the tamer natives we employed
to hew and draw, but did not call them slaves.
Some say this was our error. Others claim

we were too slow to make them citizens;
we might have made them Caesar's bravest legions.
This is a matter for historians,
or old beards in the Senate to wag over,
not pertinent to us these many years.

But here and there the land was poor and starved,
which, though we mapped, we did not occupy,
leaving the natives, out of laziness
in our demanding it, to hold unleased
the marshy quarters, fens, the broken hills,
and all the rougher places where the whin
still thrust from limestone with its cracking pods.

They multiplied and came with open hands,
begging a crust because their land was poor,
and they were many; squatting at our gates,
till our towns grew and threw them hovelled lanes
which they inhabit still. You may distinguish,
if you were schooled with us, by pigmentation,
by cast of features or by turn of phrase,
or by the clan-names on them which are they,
among the faces moving in the street.

They worship Heaven strangely, having rites
we snigger at, are known as superstitious,
cunning by nature, never to be trusted,
given to dancing and a kind of song
seductive to the ear, a whining sorrow.
Also they breed like flies. The danger's there;
when Caesar's old and lays his sceptre down,
we'll be a little people, well-outnumbered.

Some of us think our leases have run out
but dig square heels in, keep the roads repaired;
and one or two loud voices would restore
the rack, the yellow patch, the curfewed ghetto.
Most try to ignore the question, going their way,
glad to be living, sure that Caesar's word
is Caesar's bond for legions in our need.

Among us, some, beguiled by their sad music,
make common cause with the natives, in their hearts
hoping to win a truce when the tribes assert
their ancient right and take what once was theirs.
Already from other lands the legions ebb
and men no longer know the Roman peace.

Alone, I have a harder row to hoe:
I think these natives human, think their code,
though strange to us, and farther from the truth,
only a little so – to be redeemed
if they themselves rise up against the spells
and fears their celibates surround them with.
I find their symbols good, as such, for me,
when I walk in dark places of the heart;
but name them not to be misunderstood.
I know no vices they monopolise,
if we allow the forms by hunger bred,
the sores of old oppression, the deep skill
in all evasive acts, the swaddled minds,
admit our load of guilt – I mourn the trees
more than as symbol – and would make amends
by fraternising, by small friendly gestures,
hoping by patient words I may convince
my people and this people we are changed
from the raw levies which usurped the land,
if not to kin, to co-inhabitants,
as goat and ox may graze in the same field
and each gain something from proximity;
for we have rights drawn from the soil and sky;
the use, the pace, the patient years of labour,
the rain against the lips, the changing light,
the heavy clay-sucked stride, have altered us;
we would be strangers in the Capitol;
this is our country also, no-where else;
and we shall not be outcast on the world.

1950   CP

An Irishman in Coventry

A full year since, I took this eager city,
the tolerance that laced its blatant roar,
its famous steeples and its web of girders,
as image of the state hope argued for,
and scarcely flung a bitter thought behind me
on all that flaws the glory and the grace
which ribbons through the sick, guilt-clotted legend
of my creed-haunted, Godforsaken race.
My rhetoric swung round from steel's high promise
to the precision of the well-gauged tool,
tracing the logic in the vast glass headlands,
the clockwork horse, the comprehensive school.

Then, sudden, by occasion's chance concerted,
in enclave of my nation, but apart,
the jigging dances and the lilting fiddle
stirred the old rage and pity in my heart.
The faces and the voices blurring round me,
the strong hands long familiar with the spade,
the whiskey-tinctured breath, the pious buttons,
called up a people endlessly betrayed
by our own weakness, by the wrongs we suffered
in that long twilight over bog and glen,
by force, by famine and by glittering fables
which gave us martyrs when we needed men,
by faith which had no charity to offer,
by poisoned memory, and by ready wit,
with poverty corroded into malice,
to hit and run and howl when it is hit.

This is our fate: eight hundred years' disaster,
crazily tangled as the Book of Kells;
the dream's distortion and the land's division,
the midnight raiders and the prison cells.
Yet like Lir's children banished to the waters
our hearts still listen for the landward bells.

1958   CP

25

The scar

for Padraic Fiacc

There's not a chance now that I might recover
one syllable of what that sick man said,
tapping upon my great-grandmother's shutter,
and begging, I was told, a piece of bread;
for on his tainted breath there hung infection
rank from the cabins of the stricken west,
the spores from black potato-stalks, the spittle
mottled with poison in his rattling chest;
but she who, by her nature, quickly answered,
accepted in return the famine-fever;
and that chance meeting, that brief confrontation,
conscribed me of the Irishry forever.

Though much I cherish lies outside their vision,
and much they prize I have no claim to share,
yet in that woman's death I found my nation;
the old wound aches and shews its fellow-scar.

1971   OMT

The Municipal Gallery
revisited, October 1954

Brisk from the autumn of the sunlit square,
to overbrim a day already full,
because some exhibition drew me there,
the mannered essays of the latest school,
I stumbled into history unaware,
pausing a moment in the vestibule,
among the crowding presences again,
facing disarmed the stone and metal men:

O'Leary brooding in his long bronze beard,
out of the saga now, a king remote;
the tense faun, Shaw, by Rodin's marble spared
the pitiful declension of his thought:
and Stephens only known as overheard
billowed on ether, or as what he wrote,
a small grimacing urchin looking lost,
too wry and various for any ghost:

George Russell, then, my fellow countryman,
a lad this, as of seventy years ago;
you could not tell from this slight beardless one,
that this was he who, in day's afterglow,
saw timeless creatures on gay errands run,
for there's no lettered label here to show
what scale or scope this stripling promised us;
no note here, either, of the sculptor, Hughes:

and this, the bold-jawed orator in bronze
torch of rebellion, fanned by roaring crowds—
clutching my father's hand, I saw him once,
when heaven seemed scarcely higher than the clouds,
muster his dispossessed battalions—
who guttered his bright flame in smoky feuds;
but there's no name here either: you must guess
what passions forged these features with what stress:

another, named at least, a comely face
scorched to the skull and ardour of a saint,
a legend she, of time-surmounting grace:
verse ambers her beyond all scathe or taint,
and she's safe there; though in this silent place
false patination of the flaking paint,
indifferent as weather has defaced
what should long since have been in metal cast.

And as I moved among these images,
nameless or named, still emblems of the power
that wrought a nation out of bitterness,
and gave its history one triumphant hour,
my heart, dejected, wondered which of these
may hold a meaning that will long endure,
for, see, before me, threatening, immense,
the creeping haircracks of indifference.

1954   CP

2.
Divided Ulster

William Allingham, an earlier poet from Ulster, whom John Hewitt much admired, wrote the following epigram about a hundred years ago.

> Not men and women in an Irish Street
> But Catholics and Protestants you meet.

Most epigrams are only half-truths, and this statement is far too simple to contain the whole truth about Ireland's troubles, but it does touch a nerve in the sad history of divided Ulster.

The poems in this section all reveal aspects of division and strife in Ulster's past and present.

For any Irishman

Your face, voice, name will tell
those master of such scholarship,
as the veins of a pebble
readily encapsulate
an exact geology,
the lava flows, the faults,
the glacial periods,
the sediments which formed
and grip us locked and rocked
in the cold tides that beat
on these disastrous shores.

1974   TE

Encounter nineteen-twenty

Kicking a ragged ball from lamp to lamp,
in close November dusk, my head well down,
not yet aware the team had dribbled off,
I collided with a stiffly striding man.

He cursed. I stumbled, glimpsing his sharp face,
his coat brushed open and a rifle held
close to his side. That image has become
the shape of fear that waits each Irish child.

Shock sent each reeling from the light's pale cone;
in shadow since that man moves out to kill;
and I, with thumping heart, from lamp to lamp,
still race to score my sad unchallenged goal.

1948   TE

Two spectres haunt me

Still from those years two incidents remain
which challenge yet my bland philosophy,
on this neat sheet leave dark corrosive stain,
which mars the dream of what I hope might be.
First, on the paved edge of our cinder field,
intent till dusk, upon our game, I ran
by accident against a striding man
and glimpsed the shotgun he had thought concealed.

Then, once, I saw a working man attack
a cycling sergeant. Whistle. Warning shout.
As if by magic plain-clothes men sprang out,
grappled the struggler, carried, rammed his head
against a garden wall. I watched the red
blood dribble down his brow, his limbs grow slack.

1978   KS

After the fire

After a night when sky was lit with fire,
we wandered down familiar Agnes Street,
and at each side street corner we would meet
the frequent public houses, each a pyre
of smoking rafters, charred, the floors a mass
of smouldering debris, sideboard, table, bed,
smashed counters, empty bottles, shards of glass,
the Catholic landlord and his family fled.

I walked that day with Willie Morrisey;
while I still feared all priests he was my friend.
Though clearly in the wrong, I would defend
his right to his own dark mythology.
You must give freedom if you would be free,
for only friendship matters in the end.

1978   KS

The green shoot

In my harsh city, when a Catholic priest,
known by his collar, padded down our street,
I'd trot beside him, pull my schoolcap off
and fling it on the ground and stamp on it.

I'd catch my enemy, that errand-boy,
grip his torn jersey and admonish him
first to admit his faith, and when he did,
repeatedly to curse the Pope of Rome;

schooled in such duties by my bolder friends;
yet not so many hurried years before,
when I slipped in from play one Christmas Eve
my mother bathed me at the kitchen fire,

and wrapped me in a blanket for the climb
up the long stairs; and suddenly we heard
the carol-singers somewhere in the dark,
their voices sharper, for the frost was hard.

My mother carried me through the dim hall
into the parlour, where the only light
upon the patterned wall and furniture
came from the iron lamp across the street;

and there looped round the lamp the singers stood,
but not on snow in grocers' calendars,
singing a song I liked until I saw
my mother's lashes were all bright with tears.

Out of this mulch of ready sentiment,
gritty with threads of flinty violence,
I am the green shoot asking for the flower,
soft as the feathers of the snow's cold swans.

1946   CP

35

Conversations in Hungary
August, 1969

1
In a back garden at Lake Balaton,
the lamp above the table veiled with flies,
strangers we sat to watch the full moon rise,
our host, Miklos, a friendly writer, known
from essays in a foreign magazine;
his ready English made us feel at home,
yet fresh-plucked peaches, jar of Cuban rum
confirmed the alien nature of the scene.

The eager talk ran on from book to play,
to language, politics. Then, suddenly,
he leaned to ask: You heard the bulletin?
And added, with no pause for our reply;
Riots in Northern Ireland yesterday:
and they have sent the British Army in.

2
Our friends at Balaton, at Budapest
days later also, puzzled, queried why,
when the time's vibrant with technology,
such violence should still be manifest
between two factions, in religion's name.
It is three hundred years since, they declared,
divergent sects put claim and counterclaim
to arbitration of the torch and sword.

We tried to answer, spoke of Arab, Jew,
of Turk and Greek in Cyprus, Pakistan
and India; but no sense flickered through
that offered reason to a modern man,
why Europeans, Christian, working-class,
should thresh and struggle in that old morass.

3
So failing there, we turned to history:
the savage complications of our past;
our luckless country where old wrongs outlast,
in raging viruses of bigotry,
their first infection; certain tragedy
close-heeled in hope, as by the Furies paced;
blight in the air, and famine's after-taste,
from fear, guilt and frustration never free.

Our keen friends countered with ironic zest:
Your little isle, the English overran–
our broad plain, Tatar, Hapsburg, Ottoman–
revolts and wars uncounted – Budapest
shows scarce one wall that's stood two hundred years.
We build to fill the centuries' arrears.

1969   OMT

Cultra Manor:
the Ulster Folk Museum
for Renee and John

After looking at the enlarged photographs
of obsolete rural crafts, the bearded man
winnowing, the women in long skirts
at their embroidery,
the objects on open display, the churn,
the snuff-mill, the dogskin float,
in the Manorhouse galleries,
we walked among the trees to the half dozen
re-erected workshops and cottages
transported from the edge of our region,
tidy and white in the mild April sun.

Passing between the archetypal round pillars
with the open five-barred gate,
my friend John said:
What they need now, somewhere about here,
is a field for the faction fights.

1974   OMT

The Lass of Richmond Hill; or the Royal Garden Party

I remember that Garden Party
in June of the Festival Year.
The steps down from the Parliament House
were roped-off, but we milled on the lawns,
and a military band played all afternoon
on the gravelled plateau at the top.

The Queen – Queen Mother now – appeared,
and as she stepped and turned her head, smiling,
and gently moved her right hand, as she stepped
on high heels down the stone-cascade,
I remember admiring that woman's poise,
as we crowded-in and gaped across the ropes,
hoping to catch and hoard a smile or a nod.

At that moment the uniformed band played
'The Lass of Richmond Hill',
a gay lilt and appropriate it seemed;
it was a pleasant occasion.

But I also remember wondering
if many among us had ever heard
that when the United Irishmen marched in
to Antrim town that other June day,
the young men in green jackets, the leaders,
tried to sing 'The Marseillaise',
the proper anthem for revolutions,
and none of the pikemen-peasants knew it
and few of the Belfast artisans had heard it;
so their steps got into a tangle as they straggled.
But Jemmy Hope, that reliable man
who never postured, rallied all
by striking-up 'The Lass of Richmond Hill',
which most knew anyway.
So, in step together, they swung
down the long street to meet the enemy.

The irony of it is
that this song was written
by Leonard McNally, the ugly little lawyer,
defender in the courts of the United Men,
proved by State papers, long after,
to have been a Castle informer.

How many at the Garden Party remembered
and enjoyed the complicated ambiguity.
Yet there must have been among those present,
some with forefathers in the rabble
scattered after the skirmish.

When I see the Queen Mother on the box
or in a colour supplement,
I sometimes think of 'The Lass of Richmond Hill',
of Leonard McNally and Jemmy Hope,
and you and me, my dear,
at the Royal Garden Party.

1969   TE

The coasters

You coasted along
to larger houses, gadgets, more machines,
to golf and weekend bungalows,
caravans when the children were small,
the Mediterranean, later, with the wife.

You did not go to church often,
weddings were special;
but you kept your name on the books
against eventualities;
and the parson called, or the curate.

You showed a sense of responsibility,
with subscriptions to worthwhile causes
and service in voluntary organisations;
and, anyhow, this did the business no harm,
no harm at all.
Relations were improving. A good
useful life. You coasted along.

You even had a friend or two of the other sort,
coasting too: your ways ran parallel.
Their children and yours seldom met, though,
being at different schools.
You visited each other, decent folk with a sense
of humour. Introduced, even, to
one of their clergy. And then you smiled
in the looking-glass, admiring, a
little moved by, your broadmindedness.
Your father would never have known
one of them. Come to think of it,
when you were young, your own home was never
visited by one of the other sort.

Relations were improving. The annual processions
began to look rather like folk-festivals.

When that noisy preacher started,
he seemed old-fashioned, a survival.
Later you remarked on his vehemence,
a bit on the rough side.
But you said, admit, you said in the club,
'You know, there's something in what he says'.

And you who seldom had time to read a book,
what with reports and the colour-supplements,
denounced censorship.
And you who never had an adventurous thought
were positive that the church of the other sort
vetoes thought.
And you who simply put up with marriage
for the children's sake, deplored
the attitude of the other sort
to divorce.
You coasted along.
And all the time, though you never noticed,
the old lies festered;
the ignorant became more thoroughly infected;
there were gains, of course;
you never saw any go barefoot.

The government permanent, sustained
by the regular plebiscites of loyalty.
You always voted but never
put a sticker on the car;
a card in the window
would not have been seen from the street.
Faces changed on the posters, names too, often,
but the same families, the same class of people.
A Minister once called you by your first name.
You coasted along
and the sores suppurated and spread.

Now the fever is high and raging;
who would have guessed it, coasting along?
The ignorant-sick thresh about in delirium

and tear at the scabs with dirty finger-nails.
The cloud of infection hangs over the city,
a quick change of wind and it
might spill over the leafy suburbs.
You coasted too long.

1969   UR

Neither an elegy nor a manifesto

For the people of my province and the rest of Ireland

Bear in mind these dead:
I can find no plainer words.
I dare not risk using
that loaded word, Remember,
for your memory is a cruel web
threaded from thorn to thorn across
a hedge of dead bramble, heavy
with pathetic atomies.

I cannot urge or beg you
to pray for anyone or anything,
for prayer in this green island
is tarnished with stale breath,
worn smooth and characterless
as an old flagstone, trafficked
with journeys no longer credible
to lost destinations.

The careful words of my injunction
are unrhetorical, as neutral
and unaligned as any I know:
they propose no more than thoughtful response;
they do not pound with drum-beats
of patriotism, loyalty, martyrdom.

So I say only: Bear in mind
those men and lads killed in the streets;
but do not differentiate between
those deliberately gunned-down
and those caught by unaddressed bullets:
such distinctions are not relevant.

Bear in mind the skipping child hit
by the anonymous richochet;
the man shot at his own fireside
with his staring family round him;

the elderly woman
making tea for the firemen
when the wall collapsed;
and the garrulous neighbours at the bar
when the bomb exploded near them;
the gesticulating deaf-mute stilled
by the soldier's rifle in the town square;
and the policeman dismembered
by the booby-trap in the car.

I might have recited a pitiful litany
of the names of all the dead:
but these could effectively be presented
only in small batches,
like a lettered tablet in a village church,
valid while everyone knew everyone,
or longer, where a family name persists.

Accident, misfortune, disease, coincidence
of genetic factors or social circumstance,
may summon courage, resolution, sympathy,
to whatever level one is engaged.
Natural disasters of lava and hurricane,
famine or flood in far countries, will evoke
compassion for the thin-shanked survivors.

Patriotism has to do with keeping
the country in good heart, the community
ordered with justice and mercy;
these will enlist loyalty and courage often,
and sacrifice, sometimes even martyrdom.
Bear these eventualities in mind also;
they will concern you forever:
but, at this moment, bear in mind these dead.

1972   OMT

45

from 'The Bloody Brae'

This is a dramatic poem for six voices. Hewitt referred to it in *Aquarius*, no.5, 1972. 'I wrote "The Bloody Brae" in 1936 or 1937, a one-act dramatisation of the confrontation of folk who had been caught up in the massacre at the Gobbins, Islandmagee, in 1641. The story which I invented turned into a plea for forgiveness for the wrongs of our past and tolerance between the communities. But, having been written, it lay among my papers till, nearly twenty years later, it was tidied for a broadcast production from the North of Ireland Region, and several years after that put on at the Lyric Theatre and printed in *Threshold (Vol.1, no.3)* in 1957.' The action takes place in the early eighteenth century, when the living people confront the ghosts of the past. The short passage which follows is from the earlier part of the play.

from 'The Bloody Brae'

Donald :
  I'll leave you at the far side of the burn.
  You'll only be a beagle's gowl frae home.

Margaret :
  And then the long road back for a frightened man,
  without a woman's stubborn shilty sense
  to trot him steady by the whispering places,
  the heifers nosing the bushes, the soughing trees,
  the round stone falling with a spatter of mould,
  and no one visible by, or maybe the chuckle
  the wee burn makes in the sheugh, or the cough of a fox.

Donald :
  Och, Margaret, quit your gaming. I'm not afeared.

Mary :
  Fear is a wholesome thing for a proud young man.
  The devil would never have fallen if he'd been afeared.
  These freets are useful. We'd forget the past,
  and only live in the minute, without their presence,
  the place that lacks its ghosts is a barren place.
  D'you think your father'd get such stooks of corn,
  or fill the long pits with praties, or pull strong lint,
  if ghosts, that were men once, hadn't given the earth
  the shape and pattern of use, of sowing and harvest.
  Our own best use may be as ghosts ourselves,
  not little mischievous freets but kindly spirits.

Donald :
  But, Grannie, if the minister should hear you,
  he'd name you from the pulpit to your shame.

Margaret :
  And rightly so. I never heard such talk—
  like the mad ravelings of a blackamoor,
  not a good Christian.

Mary :
>   The Book is full of ghosts
> passing through close-barred doors and bringing peace.

Donald :
>   But Saul was rebuked for wanting to speak with them.

Mary :
>   There were other ghosts than that.

Margaret :
>   But, Grannie, think. There is Heaven and Earth and Hell,
>   and each is a place by itself. Deny me that.

Mary :
>   Heaven is here, and Hell is here beside it,
>   inside, round it, all throughother together.
>   It's only a ghost that knows the place it's in.

Margaret :
>   Come on; you're deaving me with your daft words.

Donald :
>   Wait lass. I find your notions hard to follow.
>   I like my thoughts as straight as the haft of a rake.

Mary :
>   You'll maybe find the curve of a scythe makes sense
>   when you've handled it longer, Donald—

1937

3.
In the country

I'd give the collar of an Irish King
For one wet catkin jigging loosely in the spring.
('Conacre')

Although John Hewitt was born and brought
up in the streets of Belfast, he has a deep love of
the countryside and he is a keen observer of
country scenes and country people. He has a
special love for the Glens of Antrim, and for
many years he and his wife had a holiday cottage
near Cushendall.

Because I paced my thought

Because I paced my thought by the natural world,
the earth organic, renewed with the palpable seasons,
rather than the city falling ruinous, slowly
by weather and use, swiftly by bomb and argument,

I found myself alone who had hoped for attention.
If one listened a moment he murmured his dissent:
this is an idle game for a cowardly mind.
The day is urgent. The sun is not on the agenda.

And some who hated the city and man's unreasoning acts
remarked: He is no ally. He does not say that
Power and Hate are the engines of human treason.
There is no answering love in the yellowing leaf.

I should have made it plain that I stake my future
on birds flying in and out of the school-room window,
on the council of sunburnt comrades in the sun,
and the picture carried with singing into the temple.

1944   CP

The Glens

Groined by deep glens and walled along the west
by the bare hilltops and the tufted moors,
this rim of arable that ends in foam
has but to drop a leaf or snap a branch
and my hand twitches with the leaping verse
as hazel twig will wrench the straining wrists
for untapped jet that thrusts beneath the sod.

Not these my people, of a vainer faith
and a more violent lineage. My dead
lie in the steepled hillock of Kilmore
in a fat country rich with bloom and fruit.
My days, the busy days I owe the world,
are bound to paved unerring roads and rooms
heavy with talk of politics and art.
I cannot spare more than a common phrase
of crops and weather when I pace these lanes
and pause at hedge gap spying on their skill
so many fences stretch between our minds.

I fear their creed as we have always feared
the lifted hand against unfettered thought.
I know their savage history of wrong
and would at moments lend an eager voice,
if voice avail, to set that tally straight.

And yet no other corner in this land
offers in shape and colour all I need
for sight to torch the mind with living light.

1942   CP

First snow in the Glens

When the winter sky, snow-ominous, crowds in,
here at the wood's edge is the world's end;
the valley cockcrow, the bleat of sheep on the hills
hint of a wider stage, like friendly rumours,
but our immediate place is an island in time.

Chopping the twigs on a stump till the dull blood sang
(my arm beats still with the unaccustomed labour)
I too was a warm oasis-island of joy,
watching the first light flakes, and hearing the leaves,
dry on the hard ground, whisper salutation,
hearing the robin's chirr, and following
the wren's intentions in a bare thorn hedge;
for no large life, this hour, shall intersect
my patient curves; since even the hooded hag
tying her faggot of kindling, garrulous,
and John MacNaghten, that slow friendly lad,
clumping up the lane to his snares in the whins,
and at a distance, striding through slant flakes
a man, not seen before, with bag and gun,
have the same lease and something of the nature
of rocking branch, of blackbird, bluetit, wren.

1947   CP

The ram's horn

I have turned to the landscape because men disappoint me:
the trunk of a tree is proud; when the woodmen fell it,
it still has a contained ionic solemnity:
it is a rounded event without the need to tell it.

I have never been compelled to turn away from the dawn
because it carries treason behind its wakened face:
even the horned ram, glowering over the bog-hole,
though symbol of evil, will step through the blown grass
  with grace.

Animal, plant, or insect, stone or water,
are, every minute, themselves; they behave by law.
I am not required to discover motives for them,
or strip my heart to forgive the rat in the straw.

I live my best in the landscape, being at ease there;
the only trouble I find I have brought in my hand.
See, I let it fall with a rustle of stems in the nettles,
and never for a moment suppose that they understand.

1949   CP

Frost

With frost again the thought is clear and wise
that rain made dismal with a mist's despair,
the raw bleak earth beneath cloud-narrowed skies
finds new horizons in the naked air.
Light leaps along the lashes of the eyes;
a tree is truer for its being bare.

So must the world seem keen and very bright
to one whose gaze is on the end of things,
who knows, past summer lush, brimmed autumn's height,
no promise in the inevitable springs,
all stripped of shadow down to bone of light,
the false songs gone and gone the restless wings.

1936   CP

The little lough

There in a bare place, in among the rocks,
grey rounded boulders shouldered from the ground,
where no field's big enough to yield three stacks
and corn grows on a fistful of black land,
is a small narrow lake, narrow and brown,
with whistling rushes elbowed here and there
and in the middle is a grassy stone
that heron or some other wanderer
will rest on darkly. Sometimes there will rise
a squawking mallard with a startling spray,
heading far inland, that the swift eyes lose
in the low mist that closes round the day.

Tho' many things I love should disappear
in the black night ahead of us, I know
I shall remember, silent, crouching there,
your pale face gazing where the rushes grow,
seeking between the tall stems for the last
black chick the grebe is cruising round to find,
my pointing finger showing it not lost
but sheltered only from the ruffling wind.

1941   CP

The swathe uncut

As the brown mowers strode across the field
shapes fled before them thrusting back the grain,
till in a shrinking angle unrevealed
the frightened hare crouched back, the last at bay,
for even the corncrake, blind in his dismay,
had found the narrow safety of the drain.

And so of old the country folk declared
the last swathe holds a wayward fugitive,
uncaught, moth-gentle, tremulously scared,
that must be, by the nature of all grain,
the spirit of the corn that should be slain
if the saved seed will have the strength to live.

Then by their ancient ritual they sought
to kill the queen, the goddess, and ensure
that her spent husk and shell be safely brought
to some known corner of beneficence,
lest her desired and lively influence
be left to mock the next plough's signature.

So I have figured in my crazy wit
is this flat island sundered to the west
the last swathe left uncut, the blessed wheat
wherein still free the gentle creatures go
instinctively erratic, rash or slow,
unregimented, never yet possessed.

1943   CP

The stoat

Walking in the warmest afternoon
this year has yielded yet, through slopes of whin
that made the shadows luminous, and filled
the slow air with its fragrance, we went down
a narrow track, stone-littered, under trees
which with new leaf and opening bud contrived
to offer a green commentary on light;
and as we wondered silent, stone by stone,
on lavish spring, a sudden volley broke,
a squealing terror ripped through twig and briar,
as a small rabbit pawing at the air
and stilting quickly thrust full into view,
clenched on its rump a dark-eyed stoat was viced,
shaped in its naked purpose to destroy.
We stopped. I stepped across. Before a stick
could fall in mercy, its harsh grip released,
the crouched stoat vanished, and the rabbit ran
whimpering and yelping into the thick grass.
Something had happened to the afternoon;
the neighbourly benevolence of spring
was shattered with that cast of violence;
and as we turned to follow the steep track,
it seemed no inconsistent codicil,
that in the mud a broken shell should loll
in equal speckled-parts, and on a stone,
a little yolk, a golden sixpence, lay,
a fallen sun in a wrecked universe.

1950   CP

The owl

With quiet step and careful breath
we rubbered over grass and stone,
seeking that soft light-feathered bird
among the trees where it had flown.
The twisting road ran down beside
a straggling wood of ash and beech;
between us and the shadowed trees
a wire fence topped the whin-spiked ditch.
We stood and gazed: the only stir
of dry leaves in the topmost boughs;
the only noise now, far away,
the cawing of the roosting crows.
And as we watched in waning light,
our clenched attention pinned upon
that empty corner of the wood,
it seemed the quiet bird had gone.

Then when the light had ebbed to dusk
you moved a hand and signalled me:
I saw the little pointed ears
beside a tall and narrow tree.
A further signal, and I moved
in wide half-circle to surprise
that little feathered sheaf of life
that watched you watch with steady eyes.
But when I came by easy stealth,
at last, within a yard or two
the brown bird spread enormous wings
and rose and quietly withdrew.
And we were left to carry home
a sense no mortal will devised,
that, for one instant out of time,
we had been seen and recognised.

1953   CP

The watchers

We crouched and waited as the day ebbed off
and the close birdsong dwindled point by point,
nor daring the indulgence of a cough
or the jerked protest of a weary joint;
and when our sixty minutes had run by
and lost themselves in the declining light
we heard the warning snuffle and the sly
scuffle of mould, and, instantly, the white
long head thrust through the sighing undergrowth,
and the grey badger scrambled into view,
eager to frolic carelessly, yet loth
to trust the air his greedy nostrils drew;
awhile debated with each distant sound,
then, settling into confidence, began
to scratch his tough-haired side, to sniff the ground
without the threat of that old monster, man.
And as we watched him, gripped in our surprise,
that moment suddenly began to mean
more than a badger, and a row of eyes,
a stony brook, a leafy ditch between.
It was as if another nature came
close to my knowledge, but could not be known;
yet if I tried to call it by its name
would start, alarmed, and instantly be gone.

1950   CP

62

O country people

O country people, you of the hill farms,
huddled so in darkness I cannot tell
whether the light across the glen is a star,
or the bright lamp spilling over the sill,
I would be neighbourly, would come to terms
with your existence, but you are so far;
there is a wide bog between us, a high wall.
I've tried to learn the smaller parts of speech
in your slow language, but my thoughts need more
flexible shapes to move in, if I am to reach
into the hearth's red heart across the half-door.

You are coarse to my senses, to my washed skin;
I shall maybe learn to wear dung on my heel,
but the slow assurance, the unconscious discipline
informing your vocabulary of skill,
is beyond my mastery, who have followed a trade
three generations now, at counter and desk;
hand me a rake, and I at once, betrayed,
will shed more sweat than is needed for the task.

If I could gear my mind to the year's round,
take season into season without a break,
instead of feeling my heart bound and rebound
because of the full moon or the first snowflake,
I should have gained something. Your secret is pace.
Already in your company I can keep step,
but alone, involved in a headlong race,
I never know the moment when to stop.

I know the level you accept me on,
like a strange bird observed about the house,
or sometimes seen out flying on the moss
that may to-morrow, or next week, be gone,
liable to return without warning
on a May afternoon and away in the morning.

63

But we are no part of your world, your way,
as a field or a tree is, or a spring well.
We are not held to you by the mesh of kin;
we must always take a step back to begin,
and there are many things you never tell
because we would not know the things you say.

I recognize the limits I can stretch,
even a lifetime among you should leave me strange,
for I could not change enough, and you will not change;
there'd still be levels neither'd ever reach.
And so I cannot ever hope to become,
for all my goodwill toward you, yours to me,
even a phrase or a story which will come
pat to the tongue, part of the tapestry
of apt response, at the appropriate time,
like a wise saw, a joke, an ancient rime
used when the last stack's topped at the day's end,
or when the last lint's carted round the bend.

1950   CP

The witch

A bunch of wrack was hung inside the porch
with frost of salt upon it, and the man
who lived within came out and looked at it
each morning for what weather was to be.
Then he went in and blew the ashen turf
and swung the kettle over the new glow
and called to the sick woman in the bed.

He was a bearded man, with puckered face
above his sailor's jersey: but his age
was far outside a small boy's aimless guess
and not worth asking, with so many things
he had to tell of ships and foreign ports.

He'd sit outside, a dish between his feet
and drop the cleaned potatoes into it,
piling the parings on another dish,
talking of Newfoundland and Liverpool
and men he'd served with. Then he'd cross the road
and hurl the parings over the sea-wall
among the tins and splintered lobster-pots
for gulls to scatter. Then he would go in
to make the dinner, and I'd walk away
kicking a ball among the drying nets.

I saw the woman once. My mother'd sent me
to fill a bucket at the gushing pipe,
and I was coming back not spilling it.
I looked in at the seaweed in the porch
when suddenly the half-door snapped its latch,
a little figure in a faded shawl
bowed on a stick, with little skinny legs,
came shuffling out. I saw her crazy face
yellow and dirty, with brown burning eyes
like all the witches in my picture books.

I stopped in fright. She opened her creased mouth
and mumbled something that I could not hear
and didn't want to.
                    When I found my strength
I dropped the bucket and ran straight for home.

Next day the sailor would not speak to me.

1940   CP

Turf carrier on Aranmore

The small boy drove the shaggy ass
out of the yard along the track,
rutted between two drystone walls,
his errand guessed from half-built stack.
Barefoot he tripped behind its tail,
too shy to lag and stride with us:
an older lad would match our pace
and snatch some topic to discuss.
He swung his switch, a salley rod,
his bleached head glinting in the sun,
but only flicked his ragged thighs
and pattered nonchalantly on.

We spoke no word. The boy, the ass,
the rutted path across the bare
unprofitable mountainside,
were native to this Druid air.
But, as we followed, rag and patch,
the string which braced each splintered creel,
the bald, rubbed flank, the hooves unshod,
growing awry and down-at-heel,
so woke our pity, I pronounced
a bitter sentence to condemn
the land that bred such boys and beasts
to starve the beauty out of them.

The small boy heard, not quite my words,
but, rather say, my angry tone;
a bright blush warmed his sunburnt neck;
he struck a sharp and jolting bone,
and turned the ass with prod and cry
through the first gap that caught his glance,
although the ruts roamed on ahead
to meet the bog's black-trenched expanse,

misjudging my intent and sure
that we were proud and critical.
Your father's beast is very dear,
if you are poor, if you are small.

1944   CP

Mary Hagan, Islandmagee, 1919

She wore high sea-boots and a wave-dowsed skirt,
a man's cloth cap, a jersey, her forearms freckled,
wind-roughened her strong face; with the men
she hauled the boat up, harsh upon the shingle,
and as they hauled they called out to each other,
she coarse as the rest. A skinny twelve-year-old,
pale from the city, watched this marvellous
creature, large-eyed, from my sun-warmed boulder.

I cannot remember her at any time
tossing the lapped hay, urging home the cattle,
or stepping out on a Sunday: she exists
in that one posture, knuckles on the gunwale,
the great boots crackling on the bladder-wrack;
one with Grace Darling, one with Granuaile.

1973   OMT

Minotaur

What savage world is this when folk to live
must lace their boots and walk across the sea,
or gut their summers with the herring fleet,
spending their senses, wearing bone and hide
on the hard harvest beds or hefts of picks
and posting life in little packets home?

We hurried to the pier to catch the boat,
Willy Bonar's boat that goes to Aranmore,
were early, waited sitting on a box
with dry claws in the corner. Down the steps
the green tide struck and fell in little rills,
and the rope tautened, tethered to the boat
below us rocking as its ribs were slapped
and tiny worms of light made scribbling dance
flickering along the curving underside.

The long bare quay was empty and the rails
truckless and rusted. Then a young man came
lively and trim, his left hand in his pocket,
hatless with flagging flannels to his shoes,
nodded good day and slippered down the steps,
stretched to the boat and lightly leaped on board,
shifted a hatch and tinkered in the square
of hollow deck, his shoulders out of sight.

Gazing to sea we saw a moving shape
too slow for shag and much too far away,
lost in the dip and trough, but coming in
with clearer definition gradually:
a small boat with two figures at the stern,
a dirty sail upon a stumpy mast.

Our lazy glances swung to watch the sky,
a sprawl of bundled clouds that carried rain
from the high bulk of Aranmore across
the flat green islands that lie in between
our rocky world's edge and that misted shape
and must be threaded through on a rolling swell.

The boat approached ... an old man and a girl ...
the sail was lowered, and a splashing oar
geared its momentum with familiar skill.
It bumped the steps, was tied, and they came up
after a parley with the lad who now
had found a tongue beyond mere courtesies.
They stopped with us and passed the time of day,
located us by speech, although we lacked
the lilting Irish phrase, as Irish too;
and talked a little of the distant war,
and if our house still stood and how we'd fared:
then hurried off, the old man with a box
and the young girl with hat and leather case,
her Midland destination on her lips
and twenty island years on hands and cheeks.

We rose and moved a little. Bonar next,
a broad faced fellow with a grey cloth cap,
saluted us, and so we went aboard
avoiding cones of rope and the lashed mast.
They spoke some words. The young man nimbly stretched
from the high bow and loosened the wet knot
round the stone pillar. Bonar with an oar
fended us off. The engine volleyed out
its random quickfire, and the stench of oil
subdued the herring smell that had become
accepted climate for our enterprise.
Then Bonar's brown left hand controlled our turn.
We passed the nearhand reef and headed clear
for the rough water running north to south,
saw to the north the great seas breaking white,
and to the south the surf on Islandcrone.

The steady engine needing no more care,
the young man sprawled at last beside the hatch,
his left arm hanging by his side, the hand
gloved but disclosing wrist of bone or wood.
We gasped at it amazed, remembering
with shock that all the nimble things he'd done ...
stretching and vaulting, tugging rope and spar ...
had been accomplished with a deft right arm
when we had watched but never realised.
We turned to Bonar whose good natured voice
grated a whisper answering our thought.
'He lost his left arm working on a farm
last year in England when a binder caught it
and nearly pulled his bloody shoulder out.
He always was a bugger for machines ... '
And then as if an afterthought he added,
'And so he can't go back like the rest of them'.

So, as we hit the channel, and the swell
swiftly thrust back the rocks on either side
and the stone houses with no stir of life
save for the silent gulls and screaming gulls,
the urgent shag that wave-high crossed our bows
and one grey heron quiet on a stone,
we held in one hurt thought the tragedy
of this harsh rim of Europe in the west.

This is a savage country for the young,
and yet the old have little bitterness,
but give a kindly word for strangers when
a child or dog reports that they are here.

They curse the barren soil, the narrow fields,
as though it were a ritual, and then
summon their years to witness that the world
has bred no better people than their kin.

1942   CP

72

Compton Wynyates, Warwickshire

for Beatrice and Ralph

The alabaster gentry, hacked and battered,
and, after, dropped into the moat:
five Tudor Comptons, one more than the four
who had spurred down the steep slope of Edgehill.

The church where they had lain, beside the great house,
was wrecked. Altar, font smashed. Not the tower;
a tower will stand against what force spills a wall,
though one might climb to tip the coping off.

Dredged up when the moat was earthed, the effigies,
in twenty years, came home, when the church was rebuilt.
Last summer I noted all, the seventeen hatchments,
the classical tablets, the box-pews. This time

I chose rather to loiter in the June sun,
musing on the squat headstones of labouring folk,
humble, enduring, among clover, buttercups,
the seeding grasses, the rain-beaded grass.

1968   OMT

On a January train journey

Gulls at the plough's tail and rooks in the fallow, the
turnip-field's empty of hoof or of bird;
only the ploughman who humours his horses, a
child with a milk can, with none for a third.

Hedges are naked and rain's in the ditches;
maybe a goat on the bank as we pass;
whin-tips are golden, but bracken is rusty, and
sheep stumble over the wind-clotted grass.

1943   SOT

Grey and white

Grey sea, grey sky,
two things are bright;
the gull-white foam,
the gull, foam-white.

1940   SOT

The sheep skull

As we came up the steep familiar lane,
famous for berries, brimmed with meadowsweet,
and bright with rose-hips in season, every rut
was stiff with frost and rigid as a bone;
and in the dead red bracken at one side
a sheep skull lay exposed, as though the year
had yielded all, had nothing more to hide,
and shaped this symbol to make all things clear.

We stopped. You poked your stick into the hole
the spine had entered, raised the sculpture up:
my left hand took it in a steady grip,
my right drew off a horn with easy pull;
then, with more labour, we dislodged its twin
and dropped the bare mask back into the grass.
One horn for powder dry when foes draw in,
and one to toast each danger as we pass.

1956   TE

76

The shortened day

After uncounted days of drought and flood,
a tired, parched season and a spate of rain
in splashing torrents dismally withstood,
autumnal peace approaches us again;
the dark streams full, the trees in disrepair,
the fields past labour ready for the spring;
but, in October light, the brightened air
brings new dimensions for our comforting.

The landmarks have not perished with our hopes;
the hills remain; the constellations turn;
the raking sun-shafts on the western slopes
shew hidden contours we have yet to learn;
and, grateful, we stand ready to obey
the brave compulsions of the shortened day.

1952   RD

4.
Memories and thoughts

This section contains mainly personal poems,
recording John Hewitt's memories of people and
places, and his reflections on human experience.
The first poem indicates the kind of readers he
hopes to find; and it suggests the quality of his
own thoughts, 'withdrawn and still'.

I write for ...

I write for my own kind
I do not pitch my voice
that every phrase be heard
by those who have no choice:
their quality of mind
must be withdrawn and still,
as moth that answers moth
across a roaring hill.

1945   SOT

Domestic help

At times we had a run of servant girls
from far-off places; one came from Conlig,
a widow's daughter, noisy, freckled, big,
whose broom whisked through the room in dusty whirls;
our cinders she called *chunners*, better swept
beneath the rugs and mats. Even more surprising,
once, round the room door where my parents slept,
poked her curl-tossing head with 'Who's for rising?'

There was another voiced her discontent
we did not dine on chicken every day
as she expected. Briefly entertaining,
their worth in work was scarcely evident,
it hardly met their pitiable pay;
my mother's fiction was they came for training.

1978   KS

The one I loved

But there was one who was the paragon,
that separated wife who wore a hat—
I wrote some lines about her, later on—
nanny and mother's help. I marvel at
the love I bear her still, remembering
the comfort she provided, and her vice,
Strong Drink, that was, to us, a sinful thing.
She came to us, and stayed and left us, twice.

The first phase finished with that fatal trip
pramming me somewhere to her tippling friends,
not to the promised park. The second ends
when her drunk husband shouted at our gate.
Though she's secure in my heart's fellowship,
my love achieved its utterance too late.

1978   KS

Betrayal

I had a nurse when I was very small—
God only knows how we afforded her,
teachers' salaries being what they were.
Yet we lacked nothing much that I recall.

I loved her well. She always wore a hat,
and prammed me out along the afternoon,
from vast adventures coming home too soon.
My careless chatter put an end to that.

I learnt to talk apace. One fated day
my father asked me if the Park was fun.
The simple truth was that our steady run
was to a crony's house a mile away,
where I was loosed from harness and let out
to tumble with my cronies on the floor,
while one of our tall seniors went next door
and brought back six black bottles they called stout
and sweeties for the children. So I told
that we had been where stout and ladies were.
My father called the nurse in, being fair,
and, though he talked a long time, did not scold.

She combed my curls next day and went away,
and I was broken-hearted for a week.
That you should always think before you speak
was something which I learnt a later day.

1966   CP

No second Troy

Later, more mother's help than mine alone,
our nurse returned, and choked affection woke;
the private games renewed, the secret joke,
each tense with eager effort to atone.

She took my hand now I had grown so much,
and walked safe places with me, never more
to knuckle on that friendly open door.
There was great comfort in that rough hand's touch;
to bath, dry, button me and comb my hair,
set straight the ship's name on my ribboned cap,
to hoist me sleepy on her shiny lap,
and hug me safely past the squeaking stair.

One night there was a row. A shouting man
leaned on our gate and called her out by name.
He hung around for hours. When no one came,
he tossed a bottle on the green sod's span
to shame our house before the neighbourhood.
This final insult was too much to take:
my father said for her sake, for our sake,
she'd better give up living here, for good.

When she was gone, my questing mother found,
beneath the thick flock mattress of her bed,
long rows of empty bottles neatly spread.
Next time the dust-cart had a clinking sound.

1966   CP

Those morning walks

But from these years I can remember still
my morning walks with father down to school;
though coming back was different as a rule,
he stayed behind with those long forms to fill,
while I rushed home, a child intent on play
with any chum I possibly might find,
though walking with my father every day
as man with man, gave me a striding mind.

We talked of everything, of Bible stories,
if they were true or false or possible?
What would Home Rule mean if it came about?
Why are some politicians known as Tories?
How many rainless days become a drought?
Could God our Father send a soul to Hell?

1979   KS

Who was C.B. Fry?

This private class for one was every day
my seminar, my university,
my asking answered in a friendly way
where heaven was? Why leaves fall from a tree?
And rainbows, tides, eclipses, falling stars?
Who was Jack London? Who is C.B. Fry?
Why are they fighting in the Balkan Wars?
Why he called some words 'fossil poetry'?–
I found *Trench* later– and what did he think
of Mrs Pankhurst? 'Bluebird' Maeterlinck?
His answers framed to stretch my inching wit
he so contrived to set my doubts at ease.
I sometimes think romantically of it
as walking with the shade of Socrates.

1979   KS

My father's ghost

My father dead, the prince among my dead,
has never come again except in dream,
unless the word that jangles in my head,
reminding me, rebuking me, 's from him;
never his palpable presence or his face,
his ink-ringed finger or his broad-splayed thumb—
yet, when I've since stood in some famous place,
I've always thought I'll tell him he must come.

It never was his wish to play planchette
or tilt a table; once I asked him why,
and I recall his confident reply,
so I have never tried. I'd rather let
my pulses keep the quiet discipline
that, if he haunts, he haunts me from within.

1949   TE

E.H. 1877-1958

She was my harbour, larder,
and my lexicon.
I ran to her for shelter.
She filled my plate with food.
I learnt my letters from the tins
she lifted from the shelf.
These twenty letters hint my debt.

1974   TE

Away match: June 1924

We crammed our compartment and crowded the windows,
denying the master all hope of a place,
the First Eleven with Tom as our scorer,
the bags on the rack of leather and baize.
Exams all over, the summer term ending,
this was the crown of my halcyon days.

Met by their captain and solemn committee,
we walked to the school in the morning sun,
changed our togs in the chilly pavilion,
gratefully swallowed the milk and the bun,
switched several names in the batting order,
and larked around till the coin was spun.

I was one of the opening batsmen,
not for my style or the runs I might make,
but rightly because I was safe and steady,
defensive, a difficult wicket to take.
The bowler handed his cap to the umpire
and loosened his arm with a slow off-break.

All has altered. That world has gone under.
Those still living are sober and staid,
retired from pulpit or general practice,
or worried and bald in some withering trade.
One, tripped-up on the rim of a scandal,
took his life when he felt betrayed.

But I remember that bright June morning,
the locals perched on the low stone wall,
the bowling-screen and, beyond in the valley,
full-leafed sycamores glittering tall,
and, far away in the Palace Barracks,
the stirring thrill of a bugle call:

the flight of pigeons, the cockcrow distant,
the bruised-grass smell from the well-spiked heel,
the pock and knock of the maiden over,
the snick to leg and the quick appeal;
the hour is noon and our score is twenty,
the bell in the tower is beginning to peal.

That age went under; disaster struck it:
we had no skills to keep it alive.
My innings' end was prophetic omen,
when what I meant for a cover-drive
shot straight through the slips like a skimming swallow
to the small swift hands of Kenny Five.

Idyllic the setting: the myth spored from paper;
our school-story values never were true:
hardly half of our team were boarders;
neither the bats nor the pads were new;
but a cricket cap somewhere in a cupboard
has the year embroidered in white on blue.

1944   TE

First funeral

Once when I was only eight or nine
and could not yet recall any
death as personal, my dead
were then a long way distant
buried in the green foot-hills, a far
journey, once a year for short legs,
I went with my mother 'to have
a look at her father's grave'.

Assured of her direction, she paced
the paths between the granite kerbs
and the twisted rods of iron, till we came
to the gilt-lettered black marble ...
While she was busy and I waited,
with only my grandfather there
the stone was quickly read,
a dark bare-headed dozen gathered
and four men put a bright coffin on clay,
two avenues away, beside
a pillar with a half-draped urn.
A small white-bearded man stepped forward,
and in the wind, the fresh west wind from
the high green hills, his beautiful voice
came gusting towards us,
Scots, and sad and terrible.

My mother standing still, whispered
'It's John Pollock of St Enoch's
I'd love him to bury me
when my time comes'.

I was only eight or nine
yet I remember the scene,
the hills, the stones, the clay,
and hearing the words, and my thinking
that what my mother said was strange,
for she would never die.

1970   OMT

Clogh-Oir : September 1971

for Roberta

Requested journey to a planned occasion,
a poet's praising, bronze-unveiling, lecture,
thrust us, not expecting, through small places
where you had lived sharp fragments of your past,
your childhood past, among grave strangers,
urged country-air and fare for your pale face,
from the grey street a farmhouse holiday;
but found it not all skipping in the sun,
fenced with unanticipated tasks,
helping about the place, with the new baby,
dishes to scour, bed-making, hearth to sweep;
Sunday trap-drive to Meeting over a shop,
where, starched with faith, a stiff sect rallied:
so you recalled as road's turn woke,
shop-name, corner, signpost, milestone noted.

As we threaded, beads on our brisk line,
the folk-rhyme place-names, Augher, Clogher,
we paused at Clogher, short of Fivemiletown,
and strolled uphill its long tidy street
to Saint Macartan's, that plain church,
early eighteenth century, Anglican,
with walled churchyard's battered crosses; inside
the inner porch, papered with prints, frames, faces,
Clogh-Oir, stripped of its gold, oracle-
stone kings once heeded, one of the Three
Sacred Stones when queens sunned at Ailech.

Time truant, all the past forgathered,
myth, legend, history, yours, mine, ours,
but, strongest whisper, it was your own
that answered you, and stirred for me, with love,
who seldom name such stirrings, or yield words
for the dialectic of the heart.

Standing there, I saw the lonely child
with the black tossing head, the dark brows,
as intense and definite as now,
as palpable, now, musing by my side,
close in a vivid murmuring congregation
among queens, heroes, bards, kneeling peasants,
immortally assembled, that child's face
known before time struck, known forever,
stuff of the fabric whereof I am made.

1971   OMT

Sonnets for Roberta (1954)

1

How have I served you? I have let you waste
the substance of your summer on my mood;
the image of the woman is defaced,
and some mere chattel-thing of cloth and wood
performs the household rites, while I, content,
mesh the fine words to net the turning thought,
or eke the hours out, gravely diligent,
to drag to sight that which, when it is brought,
is seldom worth the labour, while you wait,
the little loving gestures held at bay,
each mocking moment inappropriate
for pompous duty never stoops to play;
yet sometimes, at a pause, I recognise
the lonely pity in your lifted eyes.

2

If I had given you that love and care
I long have lavished with harsh loyalty
on some blurred concept spun of earth and air
and real only in some bird or tree,
then you had lived in every pulse and tone
and found the meaning in the wine and bread
who have been forced to walk these ways alone,
my dry thoughts droning always on ahead.
Then you had lived as other women live,
warmed by a touch, responsive to a glance,
glad to endure, so that endurance give
the right to share each changing circumstance,
and yet, for all my treason, you were true
to me, as I to something less than you.

1954   RD

95

From a museum man's album

My trade takes me frequently into decaying houses,
house not literally in the sense of gaping roof,
although often with the damp maps of wallpaper in the attic
and the pickle of plaster on the cellar shelf:
but house usually represented by a very old woman
who bears a name once famous for trade or wealth
or skill or simply breeding,
and is the last of that name.

Take, for instance, the tall large-knuckled woman in tweeds
whose grandfather was an artist of repute,
and had his quarrel with the Academy
and wrote his angry letters, and marginal notes
on those from his friends and patrons. (O pitiful letters,
I keep your copies safely in a metal drawer.)
Her mother had been part of the caravan
he trundled through Europe, eloquent, passionate, poor.

Now she offers us a few early copies
made in his student days when Rubens hit him
like a boy's first cigar;
a badly-cracked circular head-of-a-girl
with flowers on a balcony, from his Roman days;
a thick bronze medal from the Exposition;
and a beaded chair-cover made by her grandmother.

She will die in a boarding house.

I remember, too, the small stout woman well,
her white hair brushed up in a manner
which was then out of fashion but has been in it again,
her deafness and her gentle smile,
her way of talking as if her words
were like the porcelain in her cabinets.
The substance of her conversation has gone blurred:

something of Assisi and Siena and Giotto
and the children singing at evening
and mist coming up the valley, and, I think, bells.

I remember, too, her shelves of books;
Okey, Henry James, Berenson, Vernon Lee,
and a number of popular manuals
like Chaffers on Pottery Marks;
and the majolica plaque of a smiling head,
and the large glossy photograph of Mussolini
on the mantlepiece.

She was a widow, and I remember thinking it odd
that she displayed no photograph of her nephew
who was at that time a Cabinet Minister.

She died later at another address,
and left us her ceramics, but her books were to be
divided among the friends who used to come in
for an evening's bridge in the winter—
That is, all except the green-bound Chaffers
which came to us with the ceramics.

Another, younger, a spinster, led me up to an attic,
offering antlered heads, and a ship in a bottle,
and an ivory rickshaw model.

She panted a little after climbing the stairs,
and sat on a leather trunk to get her breath,
and pointed out a golden photograph
of her tall brother who died of a fever in Siam
after his first leave home.

She was giving up the house to go and live
in a larger one among trees, left by her aunt,
and in the family at least two hundred years.

I selected a rough-edged book in wooden covers,
watercolours on worm-holed rice paper, with unstuck silk
—a series of Chinese tortures of prisoners.

1944   CP

As you like it

The hurried meeting called for Law Reform
assembled slowly. Someone fetched the key,
and there were four of us, for twenty minutes,
setting the chairs in order, clearing tables.
The friendly chairman introduced himself,
found us an ash-tray, shewed us circulars
not yet despatched, which summed its decent aim.

When half a dozen dribbled in, it started.
Thanking us two as representative
of those who'd rallied to last year's appeal,
the chairman outlined why we'd come together,
called for the dapper secretary's report.
That neat man with the black moustache went through
the correspondence briskly, the replies,
refusals blunt or sharp, evasions bland
from those who wanted time to reconsider,
since to some ascending public men
our project had its queasy overtones;
posters, petitions; arguments for both
and cautious warnings; deputation, letters
to editors or paid advertisements,
and which might be the more immediate use.

We studied our associates, strange till now;
the tall man like a burly front row forward,
the quiet workingman with collar and tie,
that fat lad whose brave jokes gave light and air,
the whispering friends who shared some private gossip,
those silent by the window ... It could have been
some sports committee, a debating club ...

Then two slim girls in slacks came clomping in
on those high hooves they love now, with bare arms
and little golden chains about their throats.

I tried to place them unsuccessfully,
not among any urgent for reform –
in my long days I've learned the stereotypes,
for civil rights, for workers' unity,
for the free mind against the book-shut mind,
for rage against oppression somewhere else –
Which of these urges I could not decide
impelled these youngsters, till, at last, they spoke
with rough-rasped workshop voices – they were lads
linking with us against our laggard law
which leaves them unpermitted, out-of-step.

I thought instinctive that they posed an image
not to our serious purpose, giggling, coy ...
I have some feeling for the loneliness,
for the pathos of the homosexual,
friendless among the hugging families,
waiting, with frustrate hope, for one to love
whose destiny's the same; the furtive posture
poised against rebuff, against tabu.

Here was no protest powered by indignation.
This was play-acting; this was dressing up,
hardly amusing, childish, dissonant.

Yet, as my thought swerved, suddenly I recalled
the great boy-actors of the Bankside Globe
I'd read about but scarcely visualised,
tripping their maiden-steps to marvellous verse
that Shakespeare, Jonson, Webster wrote for them.
That dark chap there could have been Celia,
his fair friend, heart-high sportive Rosalind,
boy playing love-sick lass disguised as boy,
with all those sparking ambiguities;
but that dimension's lost. They have no play
save what they wring from their wry circumstance,
though this town still has bloody tragedies.

100

And, if it seems like farce, I am unfair;
their brittle miming primes my resolution
to pin my stubborn pledge to principle.
They have their quaint quirks – This is one of mine.

1975   TE

On reading Terence de Vere White on Landor

He says that old men fool themselves by claiming
they have the qualities they clearly lack:
so one believes he's noble, open-handed,
wise in all ways of others, all forgiving ...
another's sure he kept the ship afloat
by his own shrewdness, till that chance wave struck.
Landor loved art and hung his walls with trash,
sat cinder-gazing, with scorched, battered hands.

Now shuffling, drifting to the terminus,
I know I'm timid, proud, intolerant,
ripe with the ready tear, too sharp of tongue,
with theories primed for every attitude
that proves me right, but surest most of this,
the man men see is not the man I am.

1973   OMT

102

For a September afternoon
of unexpected brightness

The afternoon had opened like a rose:
the fallen leaves lay still; no others fell.
Time like that golden moment when the bell
holds its round note before the dying close,
seemed being, not becoming. Even those
whose movement and direction briskly spell
the city's ordered habit, capable
and urgent, by their gestures spoke repose,
and not intention only. For this hour,
all unexpected in the failing year,
they peopled the warm world as if by right,
each natural and easy as a flower
that needs no courage and can know no fear,
because it is inheritor of light.

1953   CP

The distances

Driving along the unfenced road
in August dusk the sun gone from
an empty sky, we overtook
a man walking his dog on the turf.

The parked car we passed later,
its side-lights on, a woman
shadow in the dark interior
sitting upright, motionless.

And fifty yards farther a runner
in shorts pacing steadily;
and I thought of the distances
of loneliness.

1970   OMT

The modelled head

for Eric Elmes

My friend the sculptor modelled the large head,
cast it in polyester, metal-grained.
It did not flatter, roughing the smooth cheeks
in search for planes, declensions, light and shadow,
making a feature of the fleshy nose,
catching the eyes but coarsening the tight mouth.

When I turned it round to observe the profile,
it brought my father's face at once to mind,
dead twenty years, the sculptor never knew him,
my sober father, that just, quiet man.
So it must touch some essence, reach some truth.

Set in the public gallery with the bronze
figures and faces by accomplished hands,
it stood beyond me, representative,
a period head wearing the date of style.
There I have left it to submit to judgment;
some name it at a glance, some hesitate;
too young perhaps, expressing one mood only,
correct for the hair, the chin, the hooded eyes.

Within myself I already sense a change:
with it there I have been liberated;
my life of strong opinions, vanities,
is held contained, sealed-off from chance of time;
this was that stubborn, unforthcoming fellow,
dogmatic in assertion and dissent,
staunch democrat but curt with nodding neighbours,
short of talk's small change, in love with words;
and I am left with these alternatives,
to find a new mask for what I wish to be,
or to try to be a man without a mask,
resolved not to grow neutral, growing old.

1965   CP

105

Emily Dickinson

When I, the easy one, was hurt
as never hurt before
I fumbled back through files of verse
for one who suffered more.

But all the poets' proverbs slept
as dry as my swept brain,
save that sweet witch who knew at once
my idiom of pain.

1945   SOT

106

Substance and shadow

There is a bareness in the images
I temper time with in my mind's defence;
they hold their own, their stubborn secrecies;
no use to rage against their reticence:-
a gannet's plunge, a heron by a pond,
a last rook homing as the sun goes down,
a spider squatting on a bracken-frond,
and thistles in a cornsheaf's tufted crown,
a boulder on a hillside, lichen-stained,
the sparks of sun on dripping icicles,
their durable significance contained
in texture, colour, shape, and nothing else.
All these are sharp, spare, simple, native to
this small republic I have charted out
as the sure acre where my sense is true,
while round its boundaries sprawl the screes of doubt.

My lamp lights up the kettle on the stove
and throws its shadow on the white-washed wall,
like some Assyrian profile with, above,
a snake-, or bird-prowed helmet crested tall;
but this remains a shadow; when I shift
the lamp or move the kettle it is gone,
the substance and the shadow break adrift
that needed bronze to lock them, bronze or stone.

1955   TE

The happy man

The happy leave no clues. The frightened man
peers backward to the taws behind the door,
the shattered flower-pot, the embezzled change.
The cynic wears the laminated boot
he limped with round the twilit cinder track.
The rebel always carries on his back
the roaring master or the prim-lipped aunt.
The sprawling signature curves back in time.
But when the happy man has left the room
we only can recall the instant's spur
that woke his laughter or provoked his smile.
We cannot prove how he was taught to laugh.

1942   CP

The habit of mercy

Only that lone man in the stone tower by the rough
Western Ocean consistently holds to the tragic view.
We others have our sops and varieties of anodyne:
despair at three in the morning surrenders to sleep;

the implications of the serious bulletin are swept away
by the prim whisk of the scholar or the loose mop of the clown;
the dragging swing of the band is the quickest exit of all,
for a sentimental sadness is like a warm small rain.

Even the most thoughtful and sensitive find their comfort
in the ultimate assured triumph of the suffering God,
writhing on his cross, pegged firm by nails, and moaning,
later to be accorded victorious trumpets.

Surely, by analogy, we assert, our positive pains –
scalds, burns, disappointments, frustrations, griefs –
will earn us, properly scaled to our relative statures,
accolade, garland or medal or clasp of the hand.

Suppose, for argument's sake, that Calvary was a defeat;
God faced the permitted evil and found it too much,
not merely too much for his creatures, too much for himself –
Man's honesty's kept the forsaken cry in the record –
then there's no hope save in enduring and trying by small
gestures of love and pity to publish the habit
of mercy from man to man. For the great world beyond us
has terror and horror enough to be faced and accepted.

I had thought that the parasites gorged in the animal's tears
are sufficient challenge to any with easy answers.

1955   CP

The child, the chair, the leaf

I take the unity my senses offer
such as of birdsong out to hearing's rim
and known beyond to light's edge, moving on
and coming over, or stars reported by
men with no names to clothe their words with style,
yet which, uncoloured, pass as true as stone
or taste and texture of the well-tried leaf.

Since touch, sight, hearing and the other two
have bettered my response to what revolves
around my centre and have trenched it far
beyond the little jet that was my life,
I take without dismay what pebbles fall
or slates flick over it, knowing they will drop
through drift of depth far deeper than the self.

My world's no sphere, for there are surfaces
which fail in rondure, places when my sense
admits a quagmire or a green-slimed trough
where I lack skill to step or strength to pluck
the sucked heels upward;
yet these are part of it, of the account
that I draw up and keep for settlement.

This shook me once that one, a cripple child,
loved by no mother, given another's love
not warm with kind but aimed, deliberate,
which, in a space of months with some expense
of will and resolution, turned the wry bone
in life's way straighter, should, an hour unwatched,
strike a sharp death in squalid accident,
and all that social-love deliberate
run twelve ways wasted in th'indifferent dust:
For I could sieve no metaphor from this
would lift the heart against adversity.

110

The cripple child, not allegorical,
summons no symbol or shining archetype,
that like charged metal draws the grains of ore
to shapely pattern in its fans of force,
or even accretions palpable in bulk:
a twig snapped off by shoulder lurching past;
a straw snatched up and dropped by witless pigeon
between the pavement and the *porte-cochère;*
a smashed brick on deserted building site –
not even this last, for this has overtones
of Babylon and tablets – nor a leaf
launched into shadow from a sunny branch.

For take the reason in the falling leaf
and measure it against that falling child
and there's an atom split that opens more
than all the pounding physicists contrive.
Who'd love a leaf and tie its brittle stem
against the twig it grew from that it face
the driven crystal and survive till spring?
A wiser hand would lay it in a book:
it would lie sad there, wisp of sentiment,
a fragment of a life, no more a leaf.

Take any common object, say, a chair,
a chair compiled of leaping particles
(such is the schoolman's fiction of the day)
will last so long as needed being chair:
have I here answer to my falling child?
Dare name who needed and define the need
as one could list the uses of a chair?
Or were the spinning particles required
to ease some balance elsewhere out of line?

Let no one mock me for my ignorance;
I grip the data that my wits provide,
and try the answers: if they cancel out
that is the answer; and I know the sum.

1953   CP

111

Revenant

He has come back, as some expected, and may be heard
if you are one of us or know the password,
talking to friends in committee-rooms, any evening,
making small trials of strength to shew he is well;
they say that later he intends to visit the new branches.

Some move ponderously now, assured of their judgment,
would propose a spectacular show-down
with the officials. But he forbids all this.

Some sit smiling on benches warm in his light
and cannot be urged to stir and plan for tomorrow.

Others do not believe it is he, and stay away
ostentatiously, claiming they know the facts.

I have gone once and listened, and know it is he,
but feel he was ill advised to come back again.
This complicates the business.

                    After a week
of utter agony I had clarified my mind and braced my heart,
and from then on could have faced any circumstance,
and indeed can yet, if I hold to the stubborn truth
that he was killed, and most of us ran away.

1948   CP

A local poet

He followed their lilting stanzas
through a thousand columns or more,
and scratched for the splintered couplets
in the cracks on the cottage floor,
for his Rhyming Weavers fell silent
when they flocked through the factory door.

He'd imagined a highway of heroes
and stepped aside on the grass
to let Cuchullain's chariot through,
and the Starry Ploughmen pass;
but he met the Travelling Gunman
instead of the Galloglass.

And so, with luck, for a decade
down the widowed years ahead,
the pension which crippled his courage
will keep him in daily bread,
while he mourns for his mannerly verses
that had left so much unsaid.

1975   TE

The romantic

When the first white flakes
fall out of the black Antrim sky
I toboggan across Alaska.

When a friend falls ill
I rehearse the funeral oration;
since I am for completeness,
never having learned to live at ease
with incompleteness.

1975   RD

November park

November dusk, at four o'clock,
I walk in the deserted park;
the tight-lipped trees are still; the mist
has scarcely drawn its gauze aside
since light at eight leaked hint of day.

The season's in autumnal mood,
the epoch's end, to every sense
the cadence of the dying fall,
as empty as the bowling green
that waits, indifferent, for play.

1974   RD

Expectancy

Do all men wait like this for breaking light
or, tired of waiting, turn to stem the time
with jerking gestures and a swab of words,
till grown to numbness, they are content at last
to accept the twitching nerves and the stung lids?

Can one wait worthy, cramming his creeled hours
with fists for justice, brimmed with fair intentions,
flexing his wits deliberate with toys,
and knowing them for that, and running again
where signals beckon out or seem to beckon?

Is that old man, with all his tasks thrust by,
content, bemused, or brinked on weariness,
so drugged with rumours from the beaconed shore,
or gorged on glimpses, guesses, intuitions,
he has no will or power to do aught else?

I wait here for this light in my own fashion,
not lonely on a rock against the sky,
but as the men who bred me, in their day,
as men in country places still, have time,
working in some long field, to answer you.

1947   RD

Bibliography

Published collections of poems
No Rebel Word, Frederick Muller, London, 1948
Collected Poems 1932–1967, MacGibbon and Kee, London, 1968
The Day of the Corncrake: Poems of the Nine Glens, Glens
   of Antrim Historical Society, 1969
Out of My Time, Blackstaff Press, Belfast, 1974
Time Enough, Blackstaff Press, Belfast, 1976
The Rain Dance, Blackstaff Press, Belfast, 1978
Kites in Spring, Blackstaff Press, Belfast, 1980

Privately printed collections
Conacre, Belfast, 1943
Compass: Two Poems, Belfast, 1944
Those Swans Remember: A Poem, Belfast, 1956
An Ulster Reckoning, Belfast, 1971
The Chinese Flute Player, Lisburn, 1974
Scissors for a One-Armed Tailor: marginal verses 1929–1954,
   Belfast, 1974

Other poetry publications
Tesserae, Festival Publications, Queen's University of
   Belfast, 1967
*The Planter and the Gael (Poems by John Hewitt and John
   Montague)*, Arts Council of Northern Ireland, Belfast, 1970

Prose writings
Introduction to *Coventry, The Tradition of Change and
   Continuity*, Coventry Corporation, 1966
Introduction to *The Poems of William Allingham*, Dolmen Press,
   Dublin, 1967
*The Rhyming Weavers, and other country poets of Antrim
   and Down*, Blackstaff Press, Belfast, 1974
Colin Middleton, Arts Council of Northern Ireland, Belfast, 1976
Art in Ulster: 1, Blackstaff Press, Belfast, 1977
John Luke, (1906–1975), Arts Councils of Ireland, Belfast, 1978
'Conor's Art' in *Conor: 1881–1968* by Judith C. Wilson,
   Blackstaff Press, Belfast, 1981